DATE DUE			

RAOUL WALLENBERG

Titles in the
PEOPLE WHO MADE A DIFFERENCE
series include

Louis Braille
Marie Curie
Father Damien
Mahatma Gandhi
Bob Geldof
Mikhail Gorbachev
Martin Luther King, Jr.
Abraham Lincoln
Nelson Mandela
Ralph Nader
Florence Nightingale
Louis Pasteur
Albert Schweitzer
Mother Teresa
Sojourner Truth
Desmond Tutu
Lech Walesa
Raoul Wallenberg

North American edition first published in 1992 by
Gareth Stevens Children's Books
1555 North RiverCenter Drive, Suite 201
Milwaukee, Wisconsin 53212, USA

This edition copyright © 1992 by Gareth Stevens, Inc.;
abridged from *Raoul Wallenburg: The Swedish diplomat
who saved 100,000 Jews from the Nazi Holocaust before
mysteriously disappearing*, copyright © 1988 by Exley
Publications Ltd. and written by Michael Nicholson and
David Winner. Additional end matter copyright © 1992 by
Gareth Stevens, Inc.

Library of Congress Cataloging-in-Publication Data

Daniel, Jamie.
    Raoul Wallenberg : one man against Nazi terror / Jamie Daniel,
Michael Nicholson, and David Winner.
      p. cm. — (People who made a difference)
    Abridged version of Raoul Wallenberg / Michael Nicholson,
David Winner.
    Includes index.
    Summary: Traces the life of the diplomat who saved Hungarian
Jews during World War II and mysteriously disappeared after the
Russians occupied Budapest.
    ISBN 0-8368-0629-8
    1. Wallenberg, Raoul—Juvenile literature. 2. World War, 1939-
1945—Civilian relief—Hungary—Juvenile literature. 3. World
War, 1939-1945—Jews—Rescue—Hungary—Juvenile literature.
4. Jews—Hungary—History—20th century—Juvenile literature.
5. Holocaust, Jewish (1939-1945)—Hungary—Juvenile literature.
6. Diplomats—Sweden—Biography—Juvenile literature. 7.
Righteous Gentiles in the Holocaust—Biography—Juvenile
literature. 8. Hungary—History—1918-1945—Juvenile literature.
[1. Wallenberg, Raoul. 2. Jews—Hungary. 3. Holocaust, Jewish
(1939-1945)—Hungary. 4. Diplomats.] I. Nicholson, Michael,
1937- . II. Winner, David, 1956- . III. Nicholson, Michael, 1937-
Raoul Wallenberg. IV. Title. V. Series.
D809.S8W3265   1992
940.54'779439'092—dc20   [B]   91-19712

For a free color catalog describing
Gareth Stevens' list of high-quality
children's books, call

1-800-341-3569 (USA) or
1-800-461-9120 (Canada)

PICTURE CREDITS
Ben Uri Collection 12 (upper); Bildarchiv
Preussischer Kulturbesitz 19; W.C.
Burgard 4, 48, 54; Camera Press 23, 24,
38, 40, 42, 50 (upper); Ghetto Fighters'
House, Israel 26; Martin Gilbert 25;
Agnes Havor-Takach 12 (lower, both),
27, 37 (lower), 55 (lower); Imperial War
Museum 14 (lower); Janina Jaworska,
Warsaw 18; Jethro Films, Australia 55
(upper); Keystone Collection 8, 29, 50
(lower); Kulturgeschichtliches Museum,
Osnarruck 16; Nina Lagergren 6, 7
(upper left, lower), 8; Michael Nicholson
53, 56, 57 (upper); Polish Military
Museum, Chicago 20; Popperfoto 21, 30
(lower), 43; Raoul Wallenberg
Foundation, Sweden 7 (upper right), 33
(all), 44, 45; Tom Redman cover
illustration; Svenskt Pressfoto 57 (lower);
Statens Konstmuseer, Stockholm 59;
Tom Veres 47; Weimar Archive 30
(upper), 35; Weiner Library 13.

Series conceived by Helen Exley
Editor: Amy Bauman
Editorial assistant: Diane Laska

Printed in MEXICO

1 2 3 4 5 6 7 8 9 96 95 94 93 92

PEOPLE
WHO MADE
A DIFFERENCE

*One man
against
Nazi terror*

RAOUL
WALLENBERG

Jamie
Daniel

Michael
Nicholson

David
Winner

Gareth Stevens Children's Books
MILWAUKEE

RAOUL G.
WALLENBERG

An impossible mission

In 1944, a young man named Raoul Wallenberg left his home in Sweden on a dangerous rescue mission. He was headed for Hungary, a country controlled by Nazi Germany. The Nazis — members of the Nationalist Socialist German Workers party — wanted to rid Hungary and all of Europe of its Jewish citizens as part of a plan they called the "Final Solution." Wallenberg hoped to save as many of Hungary's Jews as he could.

By 1944, the Nazis had marched across much of Europe, destroying Jewish communities and leaving millions of people dead. Now they wanted to do the same in Hungary, where Europe's last big community of Jews still survived.

Wallenberg had been sent by his government, but he brought with him little more than courage. In his suitcase he carried a passport, a gun, money, and a secret list of names. As he traveled toward Budapest, Hungary's capital, his task seemed hopeless. For before this journey, little suggested that Raoul Wallenberg would become a hero.

"Who was this Wallenberg, the mention of whose name was enough to stir life into the half dead? . . . He was a . . . product of a family of privilege and position. Why then had this young man chosen to stride into . . . the nightmare of Budapest, 1944?"

Kati Marton,
from Wallenberg

Opposite: Raoul Wallenberg was still a young man at the time of his mission, yet he faced the Nazis alone.

Raoul's mother, Maj Wising Wallenberg, became a widow at only twenty years of age when Raoul's father died of cancer.

A privileged childhood

Raoul Wallenberg was born on August 4, 1912, into a well-respected Swedish family. The Wallenberg family included many diplomats, bankers, clergy, and military leaders. In fact, Raoul's father had been a naval officer.

Sadly, Raoul never knew his father. Raoul Wallenberg, Sr., died three months before his son's birth. But as the center of his young mother's life, Raoul did not lack love and attention. When Raoul was six, his mother, Maj (Wising) Wallenberg, married Fredrik von Dardel. Raoul soon had a brother, Guy, and a sister, Nina.

Raoul was a sensitive boy who did well in school and was well-liked. He enjoyed activities such as hiking and swimming but did not like competitive sports. Airplanes, ships, and construction always fascinated him. At nine, he read reports from his family's businesses and tried to understand them. He imagined how he would someday run these businesses.

Raoul's paternal grandfather, Gustav Wallenberg, was a Swedish diplomat. He had plans for Raoul and wanted him to have a broad approach to life. For this reason, Gustav insisted on overseeing Raoul's education and encouraged him to learn many languages. By high school, Raoul knew German, French, English, and Russian. Soon he was ready to begin university studies.

Detta kort skall för att äga gillighet ovill-
korligen vara försett med innehavarens
fotografi.

Top left: Raoul Wallenberg at the age of three with his grandfather, Gustav Wallenberg. Gustav loved to tell Raoul stories of his own grandfather and great-grandfather. Raoul called these relatives the "big men."

Above: This picture, taken for a passport, shows Wallenberg at age eleven. With his passport, Raoul traveled alone to Turkey to visit his grandfather, Gustav.

Left: Raoul Wallenberg as a twelve-year-old schoolboy.

Raoul Wallenberg loved the United States because of its openness and democratic freedoms. As a student there, he liked to hitchhike and thought it was good practice for diplomats. A friend took this picture of him on the Hudson Bridge in New York. "I went three hundred miles on fifty cents," he once told his grandfather.

A student in the United States

Gustav planned that Raoul would one day become a banker. Raoul wanted to study architecture. But both of them agreed that he should study in the United States. There, at the University of Michigan in Ann Arbor, Raoul worked hard, proving himself a top student. With his talents, modesty, openness, and good sense of humor, he quickly made a name for himself.

Raoul loved the relaxed atmosphere in the United States. He spent his vacations and summers traveling as much of the country and Canada as he could. Often, he hitchhiked because he liked the different types of people he met. But even in the 1930s, hitchhiking could be dangerous. On one trip, four men offered him a ride and then robbed him. Raoul later wrote that this experience had seemed like an adventure. His ability to remain unafraid in dangerous situations would later prove important for thousands of people.

After college, Raoul began learning commerce and banking to please his grandfather. He first went to South Africa, where he worked for a Swedish import and export firm. In 1936, he moved to Haifa, in what was then Palestine, to work at a branch of the Holland Bank. He didn't really like this work and wrote to his grandfather that he would be better suited for a job where he could take "positive action," rather than sit at a desk all day. When Gustav died a year later, Raoul decided to try a new career.

He couldn't work as an architect in Sweden because his American training wasn't accepted there. Instead, he found work with a Jewish refugee, Koloman Lauer, who ran a business importing and exporting exotic food. Raoul's job was to buy and sell foods in countries all over

". . . a very talented person, with lots of ideas. . . . Once, when Wallenberg had his arm in a sling, he made all his projects with his left arm, and his presentations were excellent."
    Richard Robinson,
    a classmate at
    the University of Michigan

"We didn't know he came from such an important, wealthy family; he never talked about that. While he was here he had to budget his money. . . . That was part of the training his family had in mind for him."
    Julia Senstius,
    teacher at Michigan State
    Normal College

9

Europe, including the Nazi-occupied countries. His knowledge of languages and his personality made Wallenberg ideal for the job. Within months, he became a director of the company, known as the Central European Trading Company.

Hitler and his "master race"

Wallenberg began working for Lauer in 1941. This was a difficult time in Europe — especially for the Jews. While working in Haifa, Wallenberg met several Jews who had come there to escape the Nazis. He listened as they told of their experiences in Germany.

Adolf Hitler came into power there in 1933. Hitler believed that certain types of people were naturally superior to others. These superior people were descended from a primitive Indo-European race called Aryans. Hitler believed that German Aryans — especially those with blond hair and blue eyes — would one day form a "master race."

Hitler thought that Jews, Slavic people, blacks, and anyone not from Europe were "subhumans." He hated anyone who was different, including people with physical or mental disabilities, but he especially hated Jews. He believed the Jews had caused Germany to lose World War I and said that they were now responsible for the country's economic troubles and its high unemployment rate.

Adolf Hitler's views were popular in Germany in 1933. The Germans were still bitter about the outcome of World War I, which had ended in 1918. They felt that the war's peace treaty had placed unfair restrictions on them. In the years after the war, Germany's economy grew so bad that its money was almost worthless. Widespread job shortages made things even worse.

By 1933, the people were willing to follow any strong leader who seemed to have solutions. Adolf Hitler was such a leader. He promised to make Germany powerful again, to rebuild the economy, and to provide jobs. So when he said that the Jews had caused Germany's problems, it was easy for the people to believe him.

Adolf Hitler was voted into power in Germany in 1933 because people thought he was a strong leader. Hitler dreamed of creating a "pure" Aryan empire to rule the world.

A history of persecution

This attitude toward the Jews was not a new idea. Anti-Semitism — as hatred of Jews is called — had been present in Europe for centuries. The problem began about two thousand years ago when a group of the followers of Jesus, who had himself been Jewish, started a religion called Christianity. After Jesus died, this new religion competed with the older Jewish faith. Christianity later became the official religion in many places, including Rome.

When this happened, Christians often turned against the Jews. They branded the Jews as "Christ-killers," a myth some people still foolishly believe. Because Jews do not believe that Jesus was the Messiah, some church leaders actually said the Jews were "in league with the devil." Where these ideas were accepted, superstitious people accused Jews of bizarre or impossible crimes. Whenever a natural disaster occurred — such as the outbreak of a dangerous disease — the Jews were blamed for it.

For centuries, then, generations of Jews had faced persecution and cruelty in Europe. Often, they were forced to leave their homelands or to live in separate areas called ghettos. Many had to wear badges and weren't allowed to own land. These people became the scapegoats for all sorts of problems.

"Mankind loves to hate. It makes us feel good and right . . . so that we can project our own anger and hostility."
Professor Ron Baker, survivor of the Holocaust

Opposite: Before World War II, Jewish culture had thrived in Europe despite years of persecution. Above, a painting captures the spirit of the Jewish family. Below, photographs offer two views of the great synagogue in Budapest. It was one of the few synagogues to survive World War II.

13

Fekete árnyék!

Jews were targets of propaganda. Above: the Jew is shown as a "black shadow" over Europe. Below: Nazis often showed Jewish men bothering blond "Aryan" women.

The Nazi onslaught

Life improved considerably for Jews during the nineteenth century as Europe modernized. Jews became active in cultural and professional life. They could participate more freely in politics. But anti-Semitism hadn't been overcome; it had only changed shape. Nothing in the Jews' long and painful history could prepare them for the intensity of the terror that faced them once Hitler came into power in Germany.

Before 1933, Jews were often harassed by people who supported the Nazis. But after Hitler was elected, the situation became much worse. Synagogues and Jewish cemeteries were destroyed. Rabbis were publicly beaten. Many people refused to do business with Jews. Jews were not allowed to teach or to take part in cultural or professional life.

It didn't stop there. As anti-Jewish signs appeared in shop and restaurant windows, Jews were randomly murdered. Publicly, the Nazis declared that Jews were "racially inferior," and in 1935, they passed laws that stripped Jews of all legal rights. These Nuremberg Laws also made it illegal for Jews and non-Jews to marry, and for Jews to own property.

The horror spreads

Nazi terror spread when Hitler decided to add more land to his empire, which he

14

called the Third Reich. In 1938, Hitler took over Austria, the German-speaking country where he had been born. Nazis in the Austrian capital of Vienna began terrorizing the city's Jewish citizens. Within a month, many Jews became so desperate that they killed themselves.

In November 1938, Nazis went on a terrible rampage against the Jews that became known as Kristallnacht, a German word that means "the night of broken glass." Throughout the Reich, Jewish shops were looted and burned, and Jews were physically attacked and even killed. Later, the Nazi government ordered the Jews to pay a fine for all the damage!

The Jews are trapped

Many Jews tried to flee to other countries, but the world turned its back on them. Many countries took in only a few of Europe's desperate Jewish refugees. The United States said it had room for no more than a few thousand; Britain said the same. The British also limited the number of Jews allowed to go to Palestine, the new Jewish homeland, which Britain controlled at the time. The tiny Dominican Republic was one of the few countries that welcomed the desperate Jews. Thus, most Jews were trapped in Europe.

Meanwhile, Hitler dreamed of conquering Europe and establishing the Third Reich across the continent. By 1939,

Nazi prejudices against Jews often relied on the idea that all Jews were rich. This Nazi cartoon suggests that Jews had control of the U.S. banks.

Ein Vorschlag zur Ordensfrage

Der „Adler der Republik" in zwei Klassen: gold und silber. Die goldene Ausgabe n. „überzeugte Republikaner", am roten Band zu tragen; die silberne Ausgabe für „auf dem der Tatsachen stehende Republikaner", am schwarz-rot-gelben Band zu tragen.

A painting captures the fear and despair that the Jews felt with the Nazis in power. By the time World War II broke out in 1939, Germany's Jews were no longer citizens. The Nazis also seized the Jews' homes and valuables, concentrated the people in ghettos, and forced them to wear badges that marked them as Jews. Such cruel acts were only the first steps in the Nazi plan to rid Europe of Jews.

his armies were the most powerful in the world. Now he used them to invade Poland. This act began World War II, the cruelest and most destructive war in Europe's history. In the years that followed, Hitler's armies conquered France, Belgium, Holland, Norway, Denmark, Yugoslavia, Greece, and most of Eastern Europe. But even as he was waging this war, Hitler was also organizing a war against all the Jewish people of Europe.

Mass murder

Hitler attacked the Soviet Union in June of 1941. At first, the German troops overwhelmed the Soviet troops they faced. Along with the troops, Hitler sent in death squads called Einsatzgruppen. Soldiers of these squads were ordered to kill every Soviet Jew they could find. In just a few months, 1.5 million Jewish men, women, and children had been brutally murdered.

In some places, entire towns were massacred. Often there were no survivors because all of the inhabitants had simply been lined up and shot. But the Nazis decided that this way of killing was inefficient, and they felt they were wasting ammunition needed for the war. They soon developed a new and more horrible way of killing.

"Wallenberg said that even he did not believe some of the atrocities until he himself was an eyewitness. He went over to a brick factory where they had over ten thousand Jews herded together into an area so small that they were forced to stand up closely packed together for five days, old people and young children alike . . . many died, just standing in the brick factory."

Iver Olsen,
War Refugee Board
representative in
Stockholm, Sweden

The Final Solution

In January 1942, a group of top Nazis gathered in Berlin to make a plan for a Final Solution for what they called the Jewish question in Europe. Among those present was Adolf Eichmann, a Nazi official who had masterminded many of the earlier Jewish massacres.

The group decided that every single Jewish person in Europe should be killed through a new, simpler method — poison gas. First, the people would be rounded up and sent by train to "death camps" that had been specially built in the German and Polish countryside. Here the Nazis built gas chambers, in which it was possible to kill thousands of people at one

time. As the Jews were killed, the Nazis took their clothes, jewelry, and anything else of value to help support the German war effort.

These death camps operated for three years. By the time they were shut down, a total of six million Jews had been murdered, and much of their unique culture had been destroyed.

The gas chambers

British prime minister Winston Churchill once called this destruction of the Jewish people a "crime without a name." Today, it is called the Holocaust. Another term for it is Shoah, a Hebrew word meaning "annihilation," or "complete destruction."

The Nazi death camps were successful in part because nothing in the Jews' history could have prepared them for such a horrible experience. When the people dared to ask questions about their imprisonment, the Nazi soldiers lied to them. Often, as the Jews were taken from their homes and put on trains, the Nazis told them they were being sent to new homes in the east. At the camps, they were told that they would have to take showers before getting settled. Once they were in the "shower rooms," the doors were locked. Instead of water, deadly cyanide gas poured in from the showerheads. Within four or five minutes, everyone in the room was dead.

The badges that Jews wore were often similar to this yellow Star of David. This hexagon had long been a symbol of Judaism — the Jewish religion. During the Holocaust, the symbol clearly set the Jews apart.

Opposite: This painting, titled The Jews' Last Road, *is the work of Waldemar Nowakowski, a survivor of the death camp at Auschwitz. It shows the heartless way in which six million Jewish men, women, and children were killed.*

This picture, called The Roll Call, *was drawn by Wincenty Gawron in Auschwitz in 1942.*

Other Jewish prisoners at the camps had to remove the bodies and burn them. At times, so many people had been killed that their bodies couldn't be burned quickly enough. In this case, they were buried in mass graves.

The Jews were not the Nazis' only victims. The Nazis butchered people wherever they went. Gypsies, Poles, Russians, and members of many minority groups were also sent to death camps. Political prisoners, religious leaders, and prisoners of war were also killed. But the Jews were the only group singled out for total annihilation, and the Nazis were intent on seeing this plan through. Officials in each Nazi-occupied country were ordered to find every Jew in their area. Any non-Jew who tried to help or hide a Jew was executed.

"Every roll call was a selection: women were sent to the gas chamber because they had swollen legs, scratches on their bodies, because they wore eyeglasses or head kerchiefs. Young SS men prowled among the inmates and took down their numbers . . . [later] the women were ordered to step forward, and we never saw them again."
Lena Berg,
Holocaust survivor

The world watches

It is often thought that the Jews went to their deaths without resistance. This isn't true. There were heroic revolts in some camps, and the Jews in Warsaw's ghetto rose up and fought heroically against the Nazis for four weeks in 1943. Jews resisted however they could, but the majority still faced the ruthless, powerful Nazis unarmed and alone within populations that were either indifferent or hostile.

As the Holocaust unfolded, most of the world did little more than stand by and

watch. The Nazis had tried to keep their crimes secret. But so many millions had been killed and so many thousands witnessed the killings that the secret couldn't be kept very long. From 1942 on, reports about what was happening to the Jews in Europe began to reach the rest of the world. But sadly, these reports were often ignored.

Sometimes the reaction was even openly hostile. In 1942, for example, Britain turned away the *Struma*, a ship full of Jewish refugees. The ship sank soon after this, and all of the 769 people on board drowned. The United States also

The world was silent as thousands of Jews were murdered every day.

21

refused to allow thousands of Jews to enter the country.

The brave few

Still, there were people who acted with great humanity during this time of indifference and persecution. All over Europe, brave citizens quietly helped Jews in spite of the Nazi threat. They risked their lives and their families' safety by hiding Jews in their homes or helping them escape. Denmark, for example, refused to accept the anti-Jewish laws; thus all but a few Danish Jews were saved. The Bulgarians simply refused to send their Jewish neighbors to the death camps, and not a single death train left the country. Even in Italy, whose leader Benito Mussolini was one of Hitler's allies, some people tried to protect the Jews.

But few deeds would be more extraordinary than Raoul Wallenberg's efforts to save the Jews of Hungary. By 1944, Wallenberg had seen much of the suffering of the European Jews firsthand, since his job directing the import-export business took him throughout Europe. Wallenberg's friends and family knew that he was disturbed by what was happening throughout Europe. He was particularly upset because, as a citizen of neutral Sweden, he felt powerless to do anything to help. But soon he would have a chance to do just that.

Hungary: the last Jews of Europe

By 1944, most of the Jews in Europe were already dead. Nearly three million had been murdered in Poland, and most of Europe's smaller Jewish populations had been wiped out. The few surviving Jews had fled, were in hiding, or were slowly dying in concentration camps.

Only one large Jewish community had been spared — that of Hungary, where 750,000 Jewish citizens still lived. But even this reprieve could not last forever. In 1944, Hitler's Nazis set their sights on this last major community. By March of that year, Adolf Eichmann began deporting the Hungarian Jews to Auschwitz-Birkenau, the largest of the death camps. There, everything was ready for the Hungarian Jews. The camp's new railroad track even carried the people within yards of the gas chambers.

Adolf Eichmann

Because he appeared so ordinary on the surface, Adolf Eichmann is probably one of history's most frightening men. In reality, however, he was far from ordinary. Eichmann's job was to round up Jews and send them to their deaths. By the time he began rounding up Hungary's Jews, he had already put to death hundreds of thousands of innocent people.

In 1932 when he joined the Nazi Party, Eichmann was not well known. With his

A Jewish boy from Czechoslovakia. Nazis murdered about 1.5 million Jewish children during the twelve years of the Holocaust.

special ability in taking care of "Jewish matters," he soon made a name for himself. He was so good at his job that by 1942 he had become the assistant to Reinhard Heydrich, the man who had planned the Final Solution.

Eichmann was proud of his position. Yet after the war, he would claim that he didn't dislike the Jews. As he saw it, he was just doing his job and obeying orders. Many Nazi officers would make the same claim. It was as if they had no sense of right and wrong. Their only goals were to please their superiors; these superiors in turn wanted to please Adolf Hitler. In turn, Hitler often reminded them of his hatred of the Jews and that he wanted to "uproot them from Europe."

As soon as Eichmann arrived in Hungary, he eagerly set about his task, calling together the country's Jewish leaders. "You know who I am," he taunted. "I am the one they call the bloodhound."

The Nazis move on Hungary

The Nazis moved into Hungary in March of 1944. Eichmann led the way, hoping to take care of the Jews there with lightning speed. By this time, his killers and the machinery of the death camps had already had years of practice.

Immediately, Jews were forced to turn over their valuables. Then they were gathered together and forced into train

Adolf Eichmann, the Nazi put in charge of the Final Solution, became Raoul Wallenberg's great enemy. Eichmann was cold-blooded about his job and boasted of the speed with which he could send thousands to their deaths.

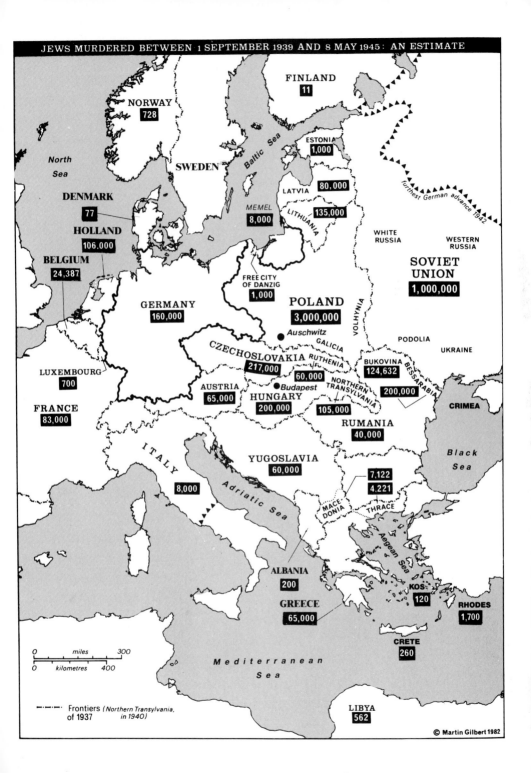

JEWS MURDERED BETWEEN 1 SEPTEMBER 1939 AND 8 MAY 1945: AN ESTIMATE

FINLAND
11

NORWAY
728

North
Sea

SWEDEN

ESTONIA
1,000

Baltic Sea

LATVIA
80,000

MEMEL
8,000

LITHUANIA
135,000

DENMARK
77

HOLLAND
106,000

BELGIUM
24,387

WHITE
RUSSIA

WESTERN
RUSSIA

furthest German advance 1942

SOVIET
UNION
1,000,000

FREE CITY
OF DANZIG
1,000

GERMANY
160,000

POLAND
3,000,000

VOLHYNIA

PODOLIA

UKRAINE

LUXEMBOURG
700

Auschwitz

GALICIA

CZECHOSLOVAKIA
217,000

RUTHENIA

BUKOVINA
124,632

60,000

NORTHERN
TRANSYLVANIA

BESSARABIA
200,000

FRANCE
83,000

AUSTRIA
65,000

Budapest

HUNGARY
200,000

105,000

CRIMEA

RUMANIA
40,000

Black
Sea

ITALY

YUGOSLAVIA
60,000

Adriatic Sea

8,000

7,122

4,221

MACE-
DONIA

THRACE

Aegean Sea

ALBANIA
200

GREECE
65,000

KOS
120

RHODES
1,700

CRETE
260

miles
0   300

kilometres
0   400

Mediterranean
Sea

LIBYA
562

Frontiers (Northern Transylvania,
of 1937   in 1940)

© Martin Gilbert 1982

All over Europe, Jews were dragged from their homes and put on trains headed for the death camps. This painting by Chris Baeckman shows a family being arrested.

"For many months now I have witnessed the suffering of the Hungarian people . . . it has now become my suffering."

Raoul Wallenberg

cars. Each train carried thousands of people. Sometimes they had to make the five-day journey to the camps with no food or water, and there were no toilet facilities for them. Many people died along the way, and the train was stopped from time to time to remove the dead.

From May 14, 1944, until July 8, the day before Raoul Wallenberg arrived in Budapest, 148 trains left Hungary for the gas chamber. The Jewish people who survived the train journey had no idea what was about to happen to them. Some were singled out to work, but most were sent straight to their deaths. About six thousand people were murdered in the gas chambers each day and their bodies were burned. The whole horrifying process took only a few hours.

The camps were like factories whose task it was to kill people. Thus, in a period of less than two months, almost 450,000 Hungarian Jewish men, women, and children were deported by the Nazis. Most of them did not survive.

Éva's diary

The terror of this time was recorded in the diary of Éva Heyman, a thirteen-year-old Romanian Jew. In her diary, Éva explained the process of being rounded up and forced onto trains headed for the camps.

In late March, she wrote that each Jew was made to wear a yellow patch so that he or she could be easily spotted. Later, on May 5, Éva wrote: "Dear Diary, now you aren't at home anymore, but in the ghetto. Three days we waited for them to come and get us.... I'm still too little a girl to write down what I felt while we waited to be taken to the ghetto. . . . The two policemen who came weren't unfriendly; they just took Agi's and Grandma's wedding rings away from them. Agi was shaking all over and couldn't get the ring off her finger."

By May 10, Éva is in the camp inside the ghetto. She tells how her grandfather, who was a druggist, gave poison to the old people who wanted to die.

Jews in hiding in a "safe house" in Budapest in 1944. Wallenberg set up many such houses.

27

May 22: "Today they announced that every head of family will be taken in [to the Dreher brewery]. Terrific screaming comes from the direction of the [brewery]. All day long an electric gramophone keeps playing the same song. . . . Day and night the noise of this song fills the ghetto."

In the last entry on May 30, Éva wrote "Dear Diary . . . I want to live." But on June 2 she was forced onto a train and sent to the death camp at Auschwitz. She was murdered there on October 17.

The United States reacts at last

By 1944, world leaders knew what was going on at the death camps. The stream of news that had been coming in about the Nazis' treatment of the Jews became a flood. Pressure was put on the allied Western forces, or Allies, to do something. By this time, U.S. president Franklin Delano Roosevelt had spoken out against the Nazis. But he had done little that might immediately help the Jews.

Many Jewish leaders in North America were angry that the United States and its officials were so slow to take action. Under pressure, Roosevelt finally agreed to set up a new organization, called the War Refugee Board, that would do what it could to help the Jews. Eventually, the War Refugee Board would prove to be a source of help and money for Raoul Wallenberg's work.

Raoul Wallenberg is chosen

The War Refugee Board needed someone to go into Hungary to see what might be done to help the trapped Jews. Officials in the United States asked Sweden for help, since it was neutral, and its government was on reasonably good terms with the German government.

Sweden agreed to help. But who should be sent? When Jewish leaders were consulted, Koloman Lauer, Raoul Wallenberg's boss in the import-export business, recommended Wallenberg.

"Here is a man who had the choice of remaining in secure neutral Sweden.... Instead Wallenberg left this haven and went to what was then one of the most perilous places in Europe ... to save Jews."

Gideon Hausner, Adolf Eichmann's prosecutor

Wallenberg was eager to accept the mission of rescuing Hungary's Jews. But he made some special requests first. He knew that time was running out and that there would be no time to check with Swedish officials whenever he had to make a decision. So he demanded diplomatic status and asked that he be allowed to issue Swedish passports to the Jews so they appeared to be Swedish. He also asked for enough money to provide safe houses and food, and to be able to bribe officials if need be.

All of Wallenberg's demands were met. He quickly prepared for his journey, as the news from Hungary grew worse each day. If he didn't hurry, Wallenberg feared, there would be no one left to save.

Wallenberg reaches Hungary

When Wallenberg finally arrived in Budapest, only about 230,000 of Hungary's Jews were still alive. The majority of them were in the capital city.

It was the summer of 1944. By this time, the Germans knew that they were losing the war. It was just a question of time. For Eichmann, the question was how many Jews he could kill before the allied armies marched into Budapest. For Wallenberg, the question was how many people he could still save. Wallenberg knew he had to work quickly. Fortunately, he had a brilliant idea.

Opposite, top: Eichmann's killers, with the help of some of Hungary's local police, continued to send Jews to the gas chambers even as Raoul Wallenberg's mission was being planned.

Opposite, bottom: These young Hungarian women are seen giving the Nazi salute. Some Hungarians welcomed the Nazi takeover.

"Wallenberg did not need to go. He went and proved that one man could make a difference."
Kati Marton
from Wallenberg

The Schutz-Pass

Wallenberg designed and printed an impressive document that looked just like a passport. It was yellow and blue like the Swedish flag and was full of official stamps and signatures. Some even had a photograph of its bearer.

Although it looked very official, Wallenberg's Schutz-Pass, or "protection pass," was a fake. It had no legal power. But it looked so official that even the Nazis were fooled. Jews who carried the Schutz-Pass were now protected, since the document made it appear that they were Swedish citizens.

Wallenberg persuaded Hungarian officials to allow him to issue five thousand passes, but he actually issued more than fifteen thousand. To do this, he sometimes had to bribe officials. Later, when printing the passes became difficult, Wallenberg began using a simpler document, but it often worked, too. Before long, other government embassies in Hungary began issuing their own passes, too.

Wallenberg knew he needed to get the passes to the people quickly. He distributed many of them himself, passing them out at the Budapest railroad station. Within weeks, thousands had been saved.

Hope

The Schutz-Pass was a sign that the Jews did indeed have supporters. Wallenberg's

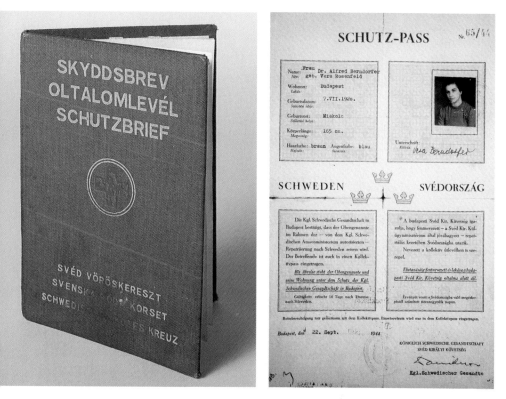

Above, left: Raoul Wallenberg's first accomplishment was to design a fake passport. He convinced the Nazis that a person carrying one of these passports was protected by Sweden.

Above, right: The phony Schutz-Pass saved thousands of lives.

Left: This piece of paper, issued by the Swedish embassy and signed by Wallenberg's colleague Per Anger, saved the life of Luise Havas. Her photo is in the top corner.

work gave a boost to people's spirits as well as saved lives. One Jewish woman recalled that the passes made people "feel like human beings again. . . ."

Wallenberg knew how important these feelings of self-respect and hope were. He wrote back to Stockholm, "The Jews are in despair. One way or another we must give them hope."

Race against time

As soon as he arrived in Budapest in July 1944, Wallenberg went to work. Within weeks of his arrival, he had a staff of four hundred people, most of whom were Jews. And somehow, he had persuaded the authorities to let his staff members work without the yellow Star of David that Jews had been forced to wear.

Wallenberg and his group, known as "Section C," worked around the clock. As a leader, Wallenberg may not have seemed impressive at first because he was small and slight. But all who met him soon realized his warmth and intelligence. He worked hard, generating energy and optimism in those working with him. Before long, even the Nazis began to respect him.

On one occasion, a deportation train was about to leave for Auschwitz. At the last minute, Wallenberg jumped onto the roof of the train, handing out his passes to the Jews inside. He ignored the Nazi

guards even when they fired their guns over his head. When he handed out the last pass, he calmly ordered all pass-holders to leave the train and walk to nearby cars marked with Swedish colors. The people were then taken to safety.

Jews were sent to the death camps on special trains. As many as one hundred people were packed into each car with no food or water. Many did not survive the journey.

Meanwhile, the United States, Sweden, and Great Britain, as well as Pope Pius XII and the International Red Cross, insisted that the Hungarian government stop the death trains. Hungary's leader, Miklós Horthy, listened to them.

Relief work

Now that the deportations had been stopped, at least for a while, Wallenberg

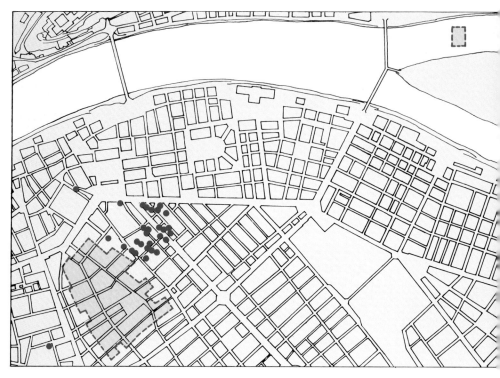

Above: This map of Budapest shows where the Jewish ghetto was in 1945. (See the shaded area outlined in red.) The purple dots show where Raoul Wallenberg had set up safe houses, which flew the Swedish flag. Here, some Jews were able to take refuge and find food and medical help.

looked for other ways to reduce the suffering. He set up soup kitchens, hospitals, and orphanages. He brought food, clothing, and medical supplies into the city and hid them for use later on.

Meanwhile, gangs of Hungarian Nazis still harassed the Jews. Many people were dragged from their homes or picked off the street. To fight this, Wallenberg set up "safe houses" where Jews with passes could live under the protection of the Swedish government. Again, other agencies followed Wallenberg's example.

After the war, one diplomat remarked that Wallenberg "accomplished feats that no other twenty diplomats in the world

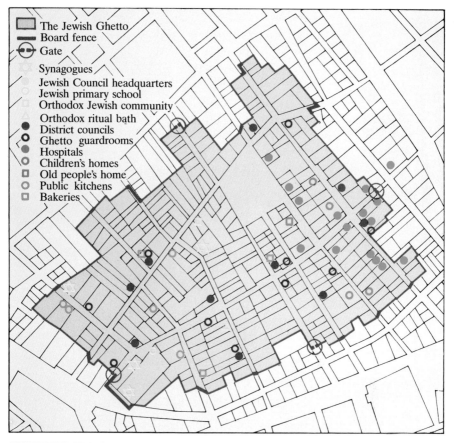

Key:

- The Jewish Ghetto
- Board fence
- Gate
- Synagogues
- Jewish Council headquarters
- Jewish primary school
- Orthodox Jewish community
- Orthodox ritual bath
- District councils
- Ghetto guardrooms
- Hospitals
- Children's homes
- Old people's home
- Public kitchens
- Bakeries

Above: A detailed plan of the Jewish ghetto in 1945. Sixty thousand people had been crammed into this cramped area.

Left: A modern picture shows the Swedish embassy in Budapest, Hungary. In 1945, Raoul Wallenberg turned it into a safe house as well.

37

Budapest was a dangerous, lawless city in the last months of the war. Armed mobs of killers roamed the streets, killing any Jews they found. Budapest was in ruins.

would even have attempted." At first, some diplomats were shocked by his unconventional methods, which included bribery, blackmail, and threats. But they soon realized that these methods worked — they were saving thousands of lives.

Bridges at high levels

Wallenberg used whatever tactics he could. One of his methods was to get to know important people who might be able to help him.

Dr. Istvan Szondy, a Budapest dentist, remembered Wallenberg, saying, "He was strong in his soul. . . . In October 1944 he opened an office here. He turned the second floor into a safe house for the Jews. There were 270 Jews living there."

Dr. Szondy also remembered that Wallenberg "tried to build bridges at high levels." One of the doctor's patients was a government official named Zoltan Bagossy. By the time Wallenberg met Bagossy, it was clear that the Allies would win the war. Wallenberg promised to help Bagossy and his family after the war if Bagossy would do what he could to help the Jews now. Later, when 250 Jews were seized from the safe house, Bagossy was able to free them with a phone call.

By October 1944, the Hungarian government was able to get the German government to remove Eichmann and his death squads from Hungary. Wallenberg thought his work had come to an end and hoped to return home by Christmas.

The Arrow Cross terror

On October 15, the Hungarian government surrendered to the Allies. But even as the people began to celebrate, the Hungarian Nazi party, known as the Arrow Cross, suddenly seized power.

The Jews left in Budapest were now threatened by violence even more terrible than before. Many Jewish people killed themselves in despair; those who didn't were locked in their homes for ten days and many starved to death.

Raoul Wallenberg didn't go home for Christmas that year as planned. In fact, he would never see his family again.

"Wallenberg never tired and was at work all day and night. He saved human lives, traveled, bargained...."
Samu Stern, Hungarian Jewish leader during the war

A Jewish family arrives at the death camp at Auschwitz. Women and children weren't selected as workers, and therefore were usually murdered a few hours after their arrival.

The staff of Wallenberg's relief office had gone into hiding. Wallenberg rode around town on a bicycle, trying to get them to come back to work. He discovered that his driver, Vilmos Langfelder, had been taken to Arrow Cross headquarters. At once, he marched into the building and demanded that Langfelder be let go. Wallenberg was so forceful that the Arrow Cross obeyed him and let Langfelder go.

Within days, Wallenberg heard that thousands of Jews were being held in a local synagogue on Dohány Street. He and the Swiss consul, Charles Lutz, demanded that Jews holding Swedish and Swiss passes be released. With great confidence, he then marched his "Swedes" out of the synagogue. Lutz followed with the "Swiss." The rest of those being held were released soon after this. It was a great victory for Wallenberg and the Jews. More than this, it was the first ray of hope since the Arrow Cross takeover.

The death marches

Adolf Eichmann returned to Budapest when the Arrow Cross took power. "I am back," he taunted the city's Jews. "Our arm is still long enough to reach you."

Eichmann could no longer rely on Hungary's railroads to carry Jews to death camps, but he had another plan. He would march them — men, women, and children — to the border. There, trains would take them on to the camps. These marches, which often took place in terrible cold and snow, became known as the "death marches." Anyone who could not keep up was immediately killed.

Wallenberg heard of Eichmann's new plan and vowed to protect his pass-holders. His office staff began to issue hundreds of letters in which they warned Hungarian officials that if they helped to persecute the Jews, they would be hanged as war criminals once the war had ended.

Unimaginable suffering

The death marches began on November 8, 1944. Children, women, and even old people had to march in the cold for days without food or water. Some froze to death. Some threw themselves into the icy waters of the Danube River. Bodies lay all along the road after the march had passed over it. The suffering of these people was unimaginable.

Miriam Herzog was seventeen years old at this time. She recalled that the Hungarian Nazis who pushed the marchers along were brutal, beating those people who couldn't keep up and leaving others to die in ditches.

Wallenberg and his helpers refused to give up on the Jews. Courageously, they drove out into the snow to bring the marchers food and encouragement. They tried to save whoever they could in any

"We were so tired that we fell down, and we slept on the earth. And in the night it was frost and in the morning we got up and many of the women were dead. We got something to eat every third or fourth day...."
Miriam Herzog, survivor of the Holocaust

On death marches, Jews were forced to march hundreds of miles in snow and bitter cold.

"Wallenberg made me feel human again. For the first time I had hope. . . . He showed us . . . that someone cared about us. And the point of it was that he came himself, he came personally.

Susan Tabor, survivor of the Holocaust

way they could. In 1980, one man who survived the marches, Zvi Eres, recorded his memories of a "foreigner" who stood on the side of the road. That foreigner was Raoul Wallenberg.

"He ordered one of his colleagues to note our names," Mr. Eres remembered. "When we reached the frontier . . . we were sent to a stable when we were told that this foreigner, Wallenberg, was trying to rescue us from the death march."

Wallenberg demanded that those holding his passes be released. As he spoke, his staff was secretly handing out

more passes to the marchers. The guards became so confused that they allowed almost anyone with an official-looking paper to go with Wallenberg. Some of the Jews were too exhausted to understand what Wallenberg wanted them to do with the passes, and he had to bluff to convince the guards.

Miriam Herzog was lying exhausted on the floor of the Swedish hut at the border where the trains left for Auschwitz. She remembered that Wallenberg was very elegant and well-dressed; after having been on the terrible march, she

Thousands of children and women died of exhaustion or were killed because they couldn't keep up on the death marches.

In the last days of the Nazi occupation, the staff at the Swedish embassy held a party to celebrate Raoul Wallenberg's success in saving so many people. They made a huge card showing famous pieces of art. The character in each piece, however, had been replaced by an image of Wallenberg with his Schutz-Passes. Here, Wallenberg appears as St. George, fighting the dragon with a Schutz-Pass instead of a sword.

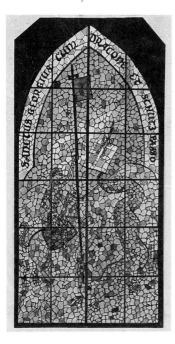

thought he looked like someone from a dream. She recalled asking, "'Who is this gentleman?' . . . and he told us, 'I want to save you all.'"

Sadly, Wallenberg could save only a small number of people from the death marches. Only thousands out of the hundreds of thousands of marchers survived. The marches finally stopped in late November 1944, only because of international protest. But the suffering was not yet over for the Jewish people.

Hell on earth

In November 1944, Hungary became completely lawless. Arrow Cross gangs roamed the streets, murdering any Jews they could find. Many Jews were taken to the banks of the Danube River, where they were shot and then thrown into the freezing water. But even the city streets were strewn with the bodies of Jews who had been killed by these vicious gangs.

Broadcaster Tommy Lapid recorded his memories of this time for a British television show about Raoul Wallenberg. He described how his mother was rescued by Wallenberg. "He was a legend among the Jews," Lapid recalled. "My mother told me that, as they were being taken down to the river, a car arrived and out stepped Wallenberg. He went after these Hungarians and protested and said these people were under his protection.

"They quarreled with him and he must have had some . . . personal authority, because there was absolutely nothing behind him. . . . They could have shot him there in the street and nobody would have known about it."

Lapid continued: "Two or three hours later, to my amazement, my mother returned with the other women. It seemed like a mirage, a miracle. My mother was there — and she was alive, and she was hugging me and kissing me, and she said one word: 'Wallenberg.' This is why I cherish his memory to this very day."

Wallenberg rushed out whenever he heard that Jewish people were in danger. In 1987, Dr. Odon Zinger, now the Chief Rabbi in Budapest, recalled how

Another section of the card made for Raoul Wallenberg shows him (at center) being given one of his own life-saving passes.

Wallenberg saved his brother along with several hundred other men.

"I asked Wallenberg for a passport for my brother, who was in a . . . work camp," Zinger reported. "He not only gave me a passport for my brother, but a hundred more for the other imprisoned workers. One day, one of the prisoners came . . . and told us the workers were being taken away. Wallenberg seized his book listing the pass-holders. . . . When we got to the camp, Wallenberg shouted out: 'How dare you deport Swedish pass-holders!'"

Wallenberg then called out the names of the pass-holders and they lined up behind him. As the passports were collected, they were secretly handed out to others who were about to be deported. That day, about six hundred people were saved with one hundred passports!

Despite such successes, the Arrow Cross often did not respect the documents. At night, they often raided houses that flew Red Cross flags. Thousands of people were dragged off, lined up, and shot.

Fear in the ghettos

The city was filled with fear — fear of the Arrow Cross gangs who raided during the night and dragged people away; fear of the Hungarian police who might come to take Jews to the railroad station; fear of German soldiers who might shoot anyone on the spot.

Once again, the Jews in the ghetto despaired. The world seemed to have forgotten them. The weather had turned bitterly cold. Starvation and disease were everywhere. People fought over what little food there was. Under these conditions, many people died during those terrible last weeks of 1944.

The fate of the Jews who were left in Budapest depended on the battle being fought between two utterly different men — Eichmann and Wallenberg. Adolf Eichmann, the Nazi backed up by thousands of soldiers and police, still wanted to kill every Jew in the city. Raoul Wallenberg, the gentleman who bore the conscience of the world, wanted just as much to see the killing stop.

Raoul Wallenberg instructing his assistants in 1944. Many of Budapest's finest community leaders worked with him. Some of these workers were saved simply because he got permission for them to stop wearing the yellow star.

Encounter with Eichmann

Eichmann wanted Wallenberg dead. He had told someone at the Red Cross office, "I will kill that Jew-dog Wallenberg." But because Wallenberg was a senior diplomat of Sweden, Eichmann couldn't hurt him.

It was amazing to think that a meeting would ever take place between these two men. But it did when Wallenberg invited Eichmann to dinner. Wallenberg thought he might be able to convince Eichmann to stop persecuting the Jews. After all, the war would be over soon. Soviet troops were only a few weeks out of Budapest.

After dinner, Wallenberg amazed his guest by attacking the Nazi beliefs. Eichmann didn't try to defend these beliefs, but said that his position with the Nazis had given him power. Because of his power, he was able to live in luxury. He enjoyed both the power and the luxury and wasn't about to give up anything.

Beyond this, Eichmann saw no reason to stop persecuting the Jews. In his opinion, the war was not over. And even if it were, for him there would be no escape once the Soviets entered Budapest. He knew he could not be pardoned for his crimes. As he rose to leave, he turned to Wallenberg, saying, "Even a neutral diplomat can meet with an accident."

A few days later, a German truck drove into Wallenberg's car and destroyed it. Fortunately, Wallenberg wasn't inside.

A drawing by W. C. Burgard shows Raoul Wallenberg talking with Adolf Eichmann. The rivals actually did meet in 1944 when Wallenberg invited Eichmann to dinner During the meeting, Wallenberg criticized Eichmann's Nazi ideas while Eichmann threatened to have Wallenberg killed.

Dead or alive?

The Soviets had almost reached Budapest in late December 1944. By this time, Wallenberg's life was in constant danger. To protect himself, he stayed in a different place every night. Still, he managed to continue his lifesaving work.

One of Wallenberg's contacts, or "bridges," became especially important now — that of Pál Szálai, an Arrow Cross member. As part of an agreement between the two men, Szálai let Wallenberg know when the death squads were going to make raids. He even provided Wallenberg with a bodyguard.

Per Anger, another Swedish diplomat, remembers his last meeting with Raoul Wallenberg during this desperate time. Anger recalled, "I asked him whether he was afraid. 'It is frightening at times,' he said, 'but I have no choice. I have taken upon myself this mission, and I would never be able to return to Stockholm without knowing I have done everything that stands in a man's power to rescue as many Jews as possible.'"

The Central Ghetto miracle

By the time the Soviets surrounded Budapest, the Arrow Cross leaders had fled. Adolf Eichmann had left as well. But before he left, he ordered his next in command to massacre all the Jews left in the Central Ghetto.

"Wallenberg was the only foreign diplomat to stay behind . . . with the sole purpose of protecting these people. And he succeeded beyond all expectations. If you add them all up, 100,000 or more people owed their lives to him."

Per Anger, Wallenberg's colleague in Budapest

Incredibly, Raoul Wallenberg was able to accomplish one last rescue. Szálai, his contact, warned him about the planned massacre. It was too dangerous for Wallenberg to speak in person to the German general who was in charge of the massacre. So Wallenberg sent him a warning: "If you do not stop this now, I can guarantee you will be hanged as a war criminal." The general backed down, and the Jews of Budapest were saved.

The Soviets arrive

In January 1945, the Soviet army entered

Budapest, and the Nazi terror ended. The Final Solution was finally brought to a halt. But in the midst of this victory, the story of Raoul Wallenberg took a tragic turn. What he had done in Budapest had made it clear that he was one of the greatest heroes of the war. He had daringly rescued no fewer than 100 thousand Jews. But instead of greeting him as a hero, the new leaders of Budapest, the Soviets, considered him a criminal.

The drive to Debrecen

Wallenberg was unaware of this new danger to himself. He was only thinking about how he would be able to help people *after* the war. He set up a small office to plan how to help find missing people and reunite families. His plans included gathering supplies of medicine, food, clothing, and everything that would be needed to get life back to normal.

When the Soviets arrived, Wallenberg decided to discuss his plans with them. He obtained permission to meet their leader in Debrecen, a town near Budapest. His assistants thought it was dangerous for him to go, but Wallenberg was hopeful about the meeting. "I am going to meet the Russians," he said. "I have money with me and will try to help the Jews."

When the Soviets came, Wallenberg went with them. He took with him a suitcase full of money for buying supplies

Opposite, top: By 1945, Hitler had lost the war. The Allies swept through Europe, freeing the few survivors of the Nazi death camps. Here, a Jewish girl eats her first hot meal in freedom.

Opposite, bottom: The Nazis continued to murder people right up to the last moment. This pile of ashes and bones taken from the ovens at one of the smaller camps was 6 feet (2 m) high.

and may also have been carrying important documents.

The day was January 17, 1945. Wallenberg smiled and waved as he was driven away. None of his friends would ever see him again.

Raoul disappears

What happened to Raoul Wallenberg after this remains a tragic mystery. It is known that, instead of listening to his plans, the Soviets arrested him. They might have thought that he was a spy.

Released Soviet prisoners reported that Wallenberg had been put in a prison in Moscow, the Soviet capital. But as weeks, months, and years went by, his many friends, including the Jews of Budapest, began to think he was dead.

The governments of the free world had ignored the suffering of the Jews until it was too late to save them. They seemed to care even less about the man who had helped them, Raoul Wallenberg.

If these governments had protested about Wallenberg's fate at once, they might have saved him. But both the Swedish government he represented, and that of the United States which had first asked him to act, failed to try very hard to find Wallenberg.

The years passed by, and the hero of Budapest became a forgotten man, hidden away in a Soviet prison. The Soviet government continued to claim it knew nothing about him. "Wallenberg is not in the Soviet Union and . . . is unknown to us," they said.

Soviet lies

But the Soviets had already given several different versions of the story. One ambassador said Wallenberg was in the Soviet Union, while the radio reported that he'd been murdered by the Nazis. Later, in 1956, the Soviet government said it had made an investigation that proved Wallenberg had never been in the Soviet Union. A year later, their foreign minister declared that he had died of a heart attack in a Soviet prison in 1947. This is the story that the Soviet government has stuck to since then.

In the following years, former Soviet prisoners testified that they had seen Wallenberg alive, and that he was sitting in a prison cell somewhere in the Soviet Union. Between 1947 and 1980, reports state that he'd been seen at no less than fifteen prisons, camps, and hospitals.

Wallenberg a spy?

Several theories exist about why the Soviets locked up Wallenberg. One is that they suspected that Wallenberg was up to more than a rescue mission in Hungary. The fact that Wallenberg's banking family had kept up its contacts with German

The Jews of Budapest had the sculptor Pál Palzai create this statue to honor Wallenberg's heroism. Sadly, Soviet soldiers hauled it away before it was unveiled, and it spent many years hidden away. It now stands outside a drug factory at Debrecen. Visitors have sometimes been told that it symbolizes the struggle against disease.

banks throughout the war may have made them suspicious.

There was also the fact that Raoul's contact at the American War Refugee Board, Iver Olsen, was a secret agent. Wallenberg didn't know this, but the Soviets probably did. Wallenberg's colleague Lars Berg believes that the Soviets suspected Wallenberg because of these contacts. "He was working with American money to save Jewish lives. I think that's why he disappeared." The Soviets were suspicious of anyone with connections to the United States. The two countries had fought Hitler together, but they were in conflict after the war.

It was many years after the war before international concern about Raoul Wallenberg began to grow. This was due largely to the efforts of Wallenberg's mother, Maj von Dardel, to locate her son.

Wallenberg's mother, Maj von Dardel (above), believed her son was alive in a Soviet prison. Below: 1987 Wallenberg memorial, Budapest.

The Budapest Jews remember

The Jews of Budapest had not forgotten the man who had helped them. After the war, they built a memorial to Wallenberg. A Hungarian sculptor created a heroic figure struggling with a large serpent. The serpent had a Nazi swastika on its head. The statue was ready in April 1948. But the night before it was to be unveiled, Soviet soldiers dragged it away. The memorial was later found in a basement in Budapest.

Wallenberg's heroism allowed Jewish life to survive in Hungary. The Jewish community in Budapest is the only large community of its kind left in Eastern Europe.

For years then, only one official reminder of Wallenberg remained in Budapest—a short street near the Danube River named "Wallenberg Street." On this street, Wallenberg's group had set up some of its safe houses. In 1987, a new Wallenberg monument, created by Imre Varga, was finally unveiled in Budapest.

The people of Israel remember

After the war, many Jewish people settled

in Israel. A number of these had originally come from Hungary. They wanted people to remember Raoul Wallenberg, so they named a street in Jerusalem for him. He is also remembered at Yad Vashem, the Israeli Holocaust Memorial, where a tree was planted in his honor. The dedication ceremony wasn't held until after Wallenberg's mother had died because she refused all along to believe that her son was dead. Wallenberg was also made Israel's first honorary citizen.

The world remembers

All over the world, people have begun to remember Wallenberg and what he did. The states of New York and New Jersey have declared a "Raoul Wallenberg Day." In 1981, Congress voted to make him an honorary citizen of the United States. Before him, only British prime minister Winston Churchill had been so honored.

The greatest memorial to Raoul Wallenberg, however, is the survival of the Jewish community of Budapest. Today, the community numbers only about 75,000 people, as compared to 750,000 before the war, but it is the only major Jewish community that remains in Eastern Europe. There, Jewish people contribute their spirit and love of learning to all areas of Hungarian life.

The Dohány Street Synagogue is still standing. Its garden is dotted with the

Above: Dr. Odon Zinger, Chief Rabbi of Budapest.
Below: People demand Wallenberg's release.

*Opposite: This portrait
of Raoul Wallenberg
was painted in 1944
by the Hungarian
artist Stanislaw
Dombrovszky. It was
given to Wallenberg's
mother in his memory.*

graves of over 2,400 Jews, although this is only a fraction of the people who died during the war. But here and throughout Budapest, there are also reminders of the community's survival. Today, Budapest's Jews celebrate their holidays without fear. The city is also home to Eastern Europe's only rabbinical school. So, thanks in large part to Raoul Wallenberg, the Jewish community of Budapest has remained a religious and spiritual center for the Jews of all of the Eastern European countries.

Never forgotten

No one can ever forget that thousands of Hungarian Jews survived because of a single man — Raoul Wallenberg. Although no one may ever know what really happened to Wallenberg, nearly fifty years after he disappeared, people still wonder. Is he dead? Could he possibly still be alive, an old man in a Soviet prison camp?

All that anyone knows for sure is that while most of the world stood by and did nothing, Raoul Wallenberg took action. His rescue mission stands out as one of the most heroic acts of the twentieth century. Whether he is alive or dead, his example will continue to provide a living inspiration for the whole world.

To find out more . . .

Organizations

Write to the organizations below for more information about the Holocaust, the life of Raoul Wallenberg, and the situation of refugees and political prisoners in different countries. When you write, be sure to tell them exactly what you'd like to know and include your name, address, and age. You should also include a stamped, self-addressed envelope for a reply.

Amnesty International
322 Eighth Avenue
New York, NY 10001

Anne Frank Institute
of Philadelphia
P.O. Box 2147
Philadelphia, PA 19103

Canadian Raoul Wallenberg
Committee
P.O. Box 8040, Station F
Edmonton, Alberta
T6H 4N7

Free Wallenberg Committee
c/o Annette T. Lantos
1707 Longworth House
Office Building
Washington, DC 20515

Raoul Wallenberg Committee
of the United States
127 East 73rd Street
New York, NY 10021

Books

The books listed below will help you learn more about the Holocaust, World War II, and Jewish customs. If you can't find them in your local library or bookstore, ask if they can be ordered for you.

About the Holocaust —

Clara's Story. Clara Isaacman and Joan A. Grossman (Jewish Publications Society)
Anne Frank: The Diary of a Young Girl. Anne Frank (Doubleday)

The Holocaust. R. Conrad Stein (Childrens Press)
The Holocaust: A History of Courage and Resistance.
    Bea Stadtler (Behrman House)
My Brother's Keeper: The Holocaust Through the Eyes of an Artist.
    Israel Bernbaum (Putnam)
A Nightmare in History: The Holocaust. Miriam Chaikin
    (Ticknor and Fields)

About Jewish History and Customs —

The Amazing Adventures of the Jewish People. Max I. Dimont
    (Behrman House)
I Am a Jew. Clive Lawton (Franklin Watts)
Introduction to Jewish History. Seymour Rossel (Behrman House)
Way of the Jews. Louis Jacobs (Dufour)

About World War II —

Invasion of Russia. R. Conrad Stein (Childrens Press)
Wartime Children, 1939 to 1945. Eleanor Allen (Dufour)
World War II. Louis L. Snyder (Franklin Watts)

List of new words

Allied Powers (Allies)
    The name that was given to the countries that fought together
    against Germany, Italy, and Japan (known as the Axis Powers)
    during World War II. The Allies included the United States,
    Canada, Great Britain, France, the Soviet Union, and other
    smaller countries.

anti-Semitism
    The practice of hating and discriminating against Jewish
    people simply because they are Jewish.

architecture
    The art and science of designing and constructing buildings.

Arrow Cross

This group, founded by Ferenc Szálasi, was the Hungarian version of the German Nazi Party.

Aryans

Originally the name given to all descendants of a people called Indo-Europeans, who, in prehistoric times, spread from central Asia into southern Asia and Europe. In the nineteenth century, the idea arose that the Aryan race was superior to all others and that Germanic people were the "purest" of the Aryan descendants. Although scientists rejected this idea, Adolf Hitler seized upon it. Hitler also narrowed the term so that it came to mean specifically people with blond hair and blue eyes — traits common among the Germanic people. It was Hitler's dream that members of this "master race" would one day rule the world.

death camps

Prison camps set up by the Nazis during World War II. Jewish people, as well as members of other religious groups, of minorities, and of anti-Nazi groups, were kept in these camps and either worked to death or killed outright.

death marches

The forced marches of Jews from Budapest to Hungary's border — a distance of about 125 miles (200 km). Nazi commander Adolf Eichmann ordered the Jews to march the distance when it became impossible to ship them out of Budapest on trains. Many people died on the march itself, and those who survived were sent to death camps.

deport

To force a person to leave the country in which he or she is living. During World War II, the Nazis deported many people from their own countries to labor and death camps in other countries that were part of the Third Reich.

diplomats
Officials who represent their home country in relations with other countries.

Final Solution
This was the code name given to Hitler's plan to kill all of the Jews in Europe. The plan was in effect from 1942 until the war ended in 1945. During this time, more than six million Jewish people were killed.

ghetto
A specific area within European cities where Jews were required to live. This word has come to refer to any area of a city in which members of a minority group live.

Hitler, Adolf (1889-1945)
Born in Austria and known for his extreme anti-Semitism, Hitler became the leader of Germany's Nazi party in 1925. He gained even more power in 1933 when he became both Germany's chancellor and its dictator. While in this position, he started World War II when he ordered German troops to attack Poland in 1939. Hitler killed himself in Berlin in 1945 when it became clear that Germany had lost the war.

Holocaust
The name given to the period from 1933 to 1945, during which Hitler put into action his plans to kill European Jews. The word Holocaust means "great destruction or loss of life."

Jew
A member of the Jewish religion; one of the Jewish people.

Nazi
A member of Adolf Hitler's political party, the National Socialist German Workers party, which was founded in 1919. The Nazi party came into power in Germany when Hitler was elected in 1933.

Palestine

An area in southwest Asia that borders the Mediterranean Sea. Also known as the Holy Land, this area was the homeland of the Jews in ancient times and has been at the center of political and religious turmoil throughout history. Today, Palestine includes sections of the modern nations of Israel and Jordan.

rabbi

A Jew who is trained as a religious leader and serves as the head of a Jewish congregation, known as a synagogue.

refugees

Persons who have been displaced from their homes or country, often because of war or political or religious turmoil there.

safe house

A place of refuge. Raoul Wallenberg's safe houses were houses claimed as the territory of Sweden. This meant that anyone staying in the house was protected by the Swedish government. These houses saved many Jews from being arrested by Nazis or members of the Arrow Cross.

Shoah

A Hebrew word that means "complete destruction." It is usually used to refer to the Holocaust.

Star of David

A six-pointed star that is the symbol of Judaism. During the Holocaust, Jews were made to wear yellow stars on their clothing to set them apart from other citizens.

swastika

A symbol that looks like an "X" with arms extending at right angles from each end. The swastika was the symbol of the Nazi party and appeared as part of the German flag while the Nazis were in power.

synagogue

A Jewish congregation. Also, the building where Jewish religious services are held, and where people can receive instruction in the Jewish faith. The word *synagogue* comes from a Greek word that means "to come together."

Third Reich

The name that the Nazi government gave itself while it was in power from 1933 to 1945. The Nazis claimed that the Third Reich would rule for a thousand years.

Important dates

1912   **May** — Raoul Gustav Wallenberg, Sr., dies at the age of twenty-three of cancer.
August 4 — Raoul Gustav Wallenberg, Jr., is born near Stockholm, Sweden.

1918   Six-year-old Raoul's mother, Maj (Wising) Wallenberg, remarries. Her second husband is Fredrik von Dardel.

1923   Raoul travels alone by train to Turkey, where his grandfather, Gustav Wallenberg, is the Swedish ambassador. By this time, Raoul has a younger half brother, Guy, and a half sister, Nina.

1931   Wallenberg travels to the United States to study architecture at the University of Michigan in Ann Arbor.

1933   **January 30** — Adolf Hitler becomes chancellor and later dictator of Germany.
Wallenberg spends the summer of this year working in Chicago at the World's Fair.

1935   Wallenberg finishes a degree in architecture and returns to Sweden. He wins second prize in an architecture competition in Stockholm, but because his degree is from an American university, he is not allowed to work as an architect in Sweden.

Wallenberg travels to Cape Town, South Africa. There he spends six months working in a Swedish-owned import and export firm.

1936   Wallenberg moves to Haifa, a city in what is now Israel, where he goes to work in a branch of the Holland Bank.

1937   **March 21** — Gustav Wallenberg dies.

1938   Raoul Wallenberg meets Koloman Lauer, a Hungarian Jew who owns an import-export business in Stockholm. Lauer hires Wallenberg to run the foreign division of the business because of his skill in foreign languages.

1939   Hitler's Germany invades Poland.
France and Great Britain declare war on Germany, and World War II begins.

1941   The United States joins in the war when the Japanese bomb Pearl Harbor in Hawaii.

1942   Plans are drawn up in Berlin for the Final Solution — the Nazi plan to kill all of the Jews in Europe.

1944   **January 22** — U.S. president Franklin D. Roosevelt sets up the War Refugee Board.
March 19 — The Germans occupy Hungary.
May 14 — Nazi official Adolf Eichmann begins mass deportations of Jewish Hungarians to the death camp at Auschwitz, Poland.
June 23 — In Stockholm, Wallenberg accepts an assignment on behalf of the War Refugee Board and the Swedish government. He is to travel to Hungary to do what he can to save the Hungarian Jews from the Nazis.

July 9 — Wallenberg arrives in Budapest, Hungary.
October 15 — The Arrow Cross seizes power in Hungary.
November 20 — The death marches begin. Over ten thousand people die on these long, harsh journeys.
December 24 — Eichmann flees Budapest as the Soviet troops move into Hungary.
December 26 — Soviet troops surround Budapest.

1945 **January 17** — Wallenberg leaves Budapest to meet with Soviet officials but does not return. It is rumored that he has been taken to a prison in Moscow.

1947 **August 18** — The Soviet deputy foreign minister, Andrei Vishinsky, claims to have no knowledge of Wallenberg's fate.

1948 **April** — The Jews of Budapest commission a statue in Wallenberg's honor. The night before it is unveiled, Soviet soldiers haul it away. It remains in a Budapest basement for years to come.

1957 Andrei Gromyko, deputy foreign minister of the Soviet Union, declares that Raoul Wallenberg died in a Soviet prison on July 17, 1947.

1979 Wallenberg's mother and stepfather die, still refusing to believe that their son is dead.
In Jerusalem, Israel, a tree is planted in honor of Wallenberg on the Avenue of the Righteous at Yad Vashem, the Israeli memorial to the Holocaust.

1981-
1986 Wallenberg is made an honorary citizen of the United States (1981), Canada (1985), and Israel (1986). By making him an honorary citizen, these nations put pressure on the Soviet Union to tell the world what has become of Raoul Wallenberg.

Index